FAST CARS

FERRARI

by Lisa Bullard

Reading Consultant:
Barbara J. Fox
Reading Specialist
North Carolina State University

Content Consultant:
James Elliott
Editor
Classic & Sports Car magazine

Capstone
press

Mankato, Minnesota

Blazers is published by Capstone Press,
151 Good Counsel Drive, P.O. Box 669, Mankato, Minnesota 56002.
www.capstonepress.com

Library of Congress Cataloging-in-Publication Data
Bullard, Lisa.
    Ferrari / by Lisa Bullard.
    p. cm.—(Blazers. Fast cars)
    Includes bibliographical references and index.
    ISBN-13: 978-1-4296-0099-6 (hardcover)
    ISBN-10: 1-4296-0099-3 (hardcover)
    1. Ferrari automobile—Juvenile literature. I. Title.
TL215.F47B85 2008
629.222—dc22   2006102217

Summary: Briefly describes the history of Ferrari and its models.

Editorial Credits
Erika L. Shores, editor; Bobbi J. Wyss, designer; Jo Miller, photo researcher

Photo Credits
Alamy/FS Agency, 7; Motoring Picture Library, cover; Phil Talbot, 15 (bottom);
    www.gerardbrown.co.uk, 22–23
AP/Wide World Photos, 6
Corbis/Car Culture, 18–19, 28–29; Sygma/Richard Melloul, 25;
    Vittoriano Rastelli, 24
Rex USA, 20–21
Ron Kimball Stock/Ron Kimball, 4–5, 8–9, 10, 14 (both), 15 (top), 26–27
SuperStock, Inc., 12–13
ZUMA Press/David Cooper, 16–17

Essential content terms are **bold** and are defined at the bottom of the
pages where they first appear.

1 2 3 4 5 6 12 11 10 09 08 07

TABLE OF CONTENTS

chapter 1

FAST AND EXPENSIVE

A shiny red Ferrari speeds down the freeway. Car lovers everywhere want one of these expensive cars.

In 1947, Italian Enzo Ferrari started a company to build race cars. Today, Ferrari makes some of the fastest cars on the road and the racetrack.

Ferrari racers at the starting line in 1957

fast fact

Many Ferraris are painted red because it's the traditional color of Italian race cars.

chapter 2

A HISTORY OF SPEED

Ferrari built the 166 MM Touring Barchetta in 1948. It showed the world a new, lightweight design for a sports car.

Ferrari sports cars quickly became popular. But the company still put racing first. The 1962 250 GTO was built to win sports car races.

fast fact

Scuderia Ferrari is the famous racing division of the Ferrari company.

In 1967, Ferrari introduced the Dino 206 GT. Unlike earlier Ferrari sports cars, the Dino's engine sat behind the cockpit. The V6 engine produced 180 *horsepower*.

horsepower — a unit for measuring an engine's power

fast fact

Enzo Ferrari thought the Dino was so different from other Ferraris that he didn't put the company name on early models.

FERRARI TIMELINE

Ferrari 250 GTO is released.

1962

1948

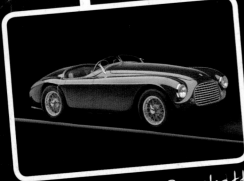

166 MM Touring Barchetta is introduced.

In 2002, the company honored its founder by building the Enzo Ferrari. This supercar's top speed is 217 miles (349 km) per hour.

Enzo Ferrari is released.

The F40 is introduced.

1987

2002

1984

2007

The 599 GTB Fiorano is released.

Ferrari Testarossa is released.

chapter 3

THE PUSH BEHIND THE POWER

Most carmakers don't use expensive V12 engines. But Ferrari puts speed first by using V12s in many of its cars.

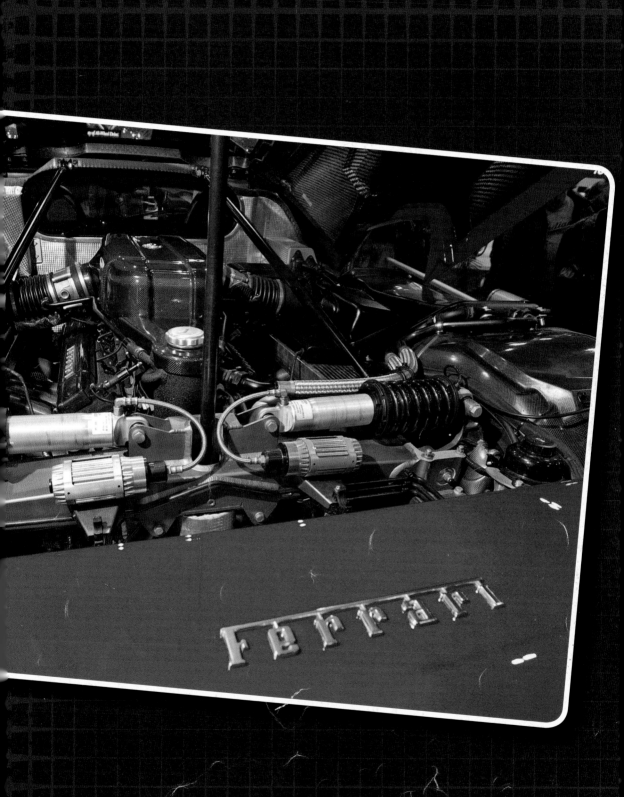

The 599 GTB Fiorano's powerful V12 engine produces an amazing 620 horsepower. It goes from 0 to 62 miles (100 km) per hour in only 3.7 seconds!

chapter 4

RACING TO STAY THE BEST

Racing remains at the heart of the Ferrari company. Ferrari wants its new sports cars to share the cutting-edge *technology* used in Ferrari race cars.

technology — the use of science to do practical things

Aerodynamic designs inspired by F1 race cars help Ferrari's F430 cruise down the road. Its F1 gearbox makes changing gears fast and smooth.

aerodynamic — built to move easily through the air

fast fact

F1 stands for Formula One racing. Ferrari race cars are Formula One.

Ferraris are among the most expensive cars in the world. Some parts are put together by hand. Ferrari also keeps prices high by limiting how many cars are made each year.

fast fact

Not just anyone can own certain Ferrari models. People who want those Ferraris must apply to the company in order to buy one.

FERRARI DIAGRAM

raked windshield

hood ornament

bumper

high-intensity headlamp

cockpit

wheel

chapter 5

THE FUTURE

Ferrari fans don't know what the company will produce next. But they know any new Ferrari will be fast, flashy, and expensive!

Ferrari 599 GTB Fiorano

GLOSSARY

aerodynamic (air-oh-dye-NAM-mik)—built to move easily through the air

cockpit (KOK-pit)—the area where the driver sits

gearbox (GEER-boks)—a car's transmission

horsepower (HORSS-pou-ur)—a unit for measuring an engine's power

technology (tek-NOL-uh-jee)—the use of science to do practical things, such as designing complex machines

READ MORE

Kimber, David. *Auto-Mania!* Vehicle-Mania! Milwaukee: Gareth Stevens, 2004.

McKenna, A. T. *Ferrari.* Ultimate Cars. Edina, Minn.: Abdo, 2002.

Mezzanotte, Jim. *The Story of Ferrari.* Classic Cars. Milwaukee: Gareth Stevens, 2005.

INTERNET SITES

FactHound offers a safe, fun way to find Internet sites related to this book. All of the sites on FactHound have been researched by our staff.

Here's how:
1. Visit *www.facthound.com*
2. Choose your grade level.
3. Type in this book ID **1429600993** for age-appropriate sites. You may also browse subjects by clicking on letters, or by clicking on pictures and words.
4. Click on the **Fetch It** button.

FactHound will fetch the best sites for you!

INDEX